Original title:

Mauve Yarns Under the Griffin Carb

Copyright © 2025 Swan Charm

Author: Johan Kirsipuu
ISBN HARDBACK: 978-1-80563-411-9
ISBN PAPERBACK: 978-1-80564-932-8

Twilight's Embrace in the Fabric of Night

In the hush where shadows play,
Stars awaken, bright and gay.
Whispers dance on velvet air,
Moonlight weaves a silver snare.

Dreams unfurl like silken sails,
Carried forth by tender gales.
Softly brushed by night's caress,
Each heartbeat finds its quiet rest.

A tapestry of darkened skies,
Where secrets linger, softly wise.
In twilight's hold, the world takes flight,
Embraced by magic's gentle light.

Secrets Untold in Whispered Threads

Beneath the stars, a tale unwinds,
In whispered threads, the heart often finds.
Woven hopes and fears alike,
In midnight's cloak, they come to strike.

Silent vows, a promise sealed,
In shadows deep, truths may be revealed.
Twisted fates and paths unknown,
In dreams and echoes, they have grown.

Softly stitched with care and grace,
Each secret held in evening's embrace.
The tapestry, both dark and bright,
Bears witness to the silver light.

Looming Shadows in the Twilight Glow

As twilight falls, the shadows loom,
Dancing lightly in the room.
They whisper tales of lost delight,
In the solemn hush of night.

Beneath the gaze of starlit eyes,
Looming figures, where magic lies.
Each flicker of the candle's flame,
Calls forth visions, wild and tame.

In every shadow, stories dwell,
Of bittersweet farewells to tell.
The night enfolds the gently spun,
Weaving dreams till the day is done.

Fables of the Night, Stitched with Care

In the fabric of soft twilight,
Fables spin to take their flight.
Glistening threads of lore entwined,
In every stitch, a tale defined.

The moon anchors tales so bright,
While stars bear witness to the night.
Each story told, a strand in time,
Woven with rhythm, spun in rhyme.

Softly whispered on the breeze,
These fables bring a sense of ease.
As they are stitched with love and care,
Embracing all in nighttime's fair.

Silken Threads of Forgotten Tales

In shadows whisper stories lost,
Of knights and maidens, fate embossed.
Through castles crumbling, time does weave,
A tapestry that none believe.

The wind carries secrets soft and low,
Where dreams take flight, and old stars glow.
With each spun thread, the past returns,
And within the heart, the ember burns.

So gather 'round, let legends flow,
From forgotten realms where memories grow.
For silken threads pull tight the night,
In stories told by flickering light.

Dreams Spun in Plum-tinted Depths

Beneath the boughs of twilight's grace,
Where whispers dance in dream's embrace.
A tapestry of plum and gold,
Awakens secrets, softly told.

Stars drip down like honeyed dew,
In realms where only dreamers flew.
With every heartbeat, visions bloom,
In velvet shadows, dispelling gloom.

So chase the echoes, wild and free,
Through corridors of memory.
For in this twilight, colors blend,
And dreams spun deep shall never end.

Chronicles of a Twilight Odyssey

When night unfolds its velvet cloak,
Upon the sea, the stars provoke.
With boats of dreams, we set our sail,
Through twilight's mist, we dare prevail.

Our hearts, like lanterns, guiding light,
Through shadows thick, a wondrous flight.
Each wave a tale, both lost and found,
In galaxies where time is bound.

To distant shores, our spirits soar,
In chronicles of lore, explore.
With each breath, our journey spins,
As twilight's odyssey begins.

Threads of Enchantment under Astral Watch

Underneath the silver gaze,
Of ancient stars in mystic haze.
The night unfurls its woven strands,
Binding dreams with unseen hands.

In silence deep, enchantments stir,
While twilight hums a gentle purr.
Each thread a promise, softly sworn,
In shadows, mysteries are born.

So let us dance in moonlit grace,
Where time and space lose their embrace.
For in this realm, beneath the light,
Threads of enchantment weave the night.

The Veil of Indigo Secrets

In twilight's grasp, the shadows dance,
Secrets whisper, as dreams entrance.
The velvet night with stars ablaze,
Hides a world in mystic haze.

Soft winds carry tales untold,
Of ancient sorrows, treasures bold.
Beneath the moon's enchanted gaze,
Hearts unravel in silent ways.

A path of indigo leads the way,
To realms where the lost find their sway.
Through echoes of time, figures glide,
In a tapestry where hopes abide.

Each thread a story, woven fine,
In the loom of fate, where stars align.
The whispers beckon, the dreams collide,
As seekers tread where shadows bide.

So wander here, where magic weaves,
In the veil of secrets, all who believe.
Let the indigo night unfold,
In its embrace, let mysteries hold.

Whims of the Celestial Artisan

Beneath the vast and twinkling sky,
An artist paints with a gentle sigh.
With strokes of light, the cosmos twirls,
Each brush a wish, as starlight unfurls.

A tapestry spun from dreams so bright,
Galaxies swirl in the velvet night.
Celestial whims on dreamer's lips,
Flow through the air in shimmering slips.

The artisan dances, heart aglow,
In realms where whispers softly flow.
A craft of wonder, of hope and cheer,
With each creation, the universe near.

From silver clouds to the moon's embrace,
Magic resides in this wondrous space.
Through cosmic laughter, we find our song,
In the hands of the artist, we all belong.

So gaze upon the starlit skies,
And let the whims of the heavens rise.
For in the night, our spirits soar,
With each celestial wish, we long for more.

In the Shadow of Winged Wonders

In twilight's hush, they take their flight,
Winged wonders bask in the fading light.
With feathers soft as morning dew,
They glide through dreams, painting the blue.

Beneath the boughs, the whispers call,
In a world where the gentle night falls.
Each flutter a tale, each beat a sigh,
Friends of the breeze, they dance and fly.

Through secret glades where the wildflowers grow,
They flit like whispers, soft and slow.
In shadows deep, their stories blend,
Nature's chosen, on them we depend.

A symphony of colors, bright and fair,
In the embrace of the evening air.
With grace they weave through the tranquil night,
In the shadow of wonders, everything's right.

So let us look to the skies above,
And cherish the gifts of winged love.
For in their flight, we find our home,
In the shadow of dreams, forever we roam.

Echoes of the Ethereal Fabric

In the silence where dreams are spun,
Echoes whisper, the magic begun.
Threads of silver, woven tight,
In the fabric of the endless night.

Mysteries linger where shadows play,
As the stars twinkle, leading the way.
Each heartbeat a pulse of the universe's core,
In the dance of time, forever explore.

Through realms unseen, we drift and sway,
In ethereal currents, come what may.
With every breath, we weave a tale,
In a world where the dreams prevail.

The fabric stretches, embracing all,
A tapestry rich, where moments fall.
Through gentle echoes, we hear the call,
Of lives entwined, in the cosmic thrall.

So trust the whispers that float through the air,
For within each echo, our souls lay bare.
In the tapestry of life, we find our art,
In the fabric of dreams, we each play a part.

Threads of Twilight Whisper

In twilight's soft embrace, we weave,
Threads of gold from dreams we conceive.
Whispers drift like autumn leaves,
As night descends, the heart believes.

Stars awaken in the sky's deep fold,
Glimmers of stories waiting to be told.
Gentle breezes carry a tune,
While shadows dance beneath the moon.

Each moment a stitch in the fabric of time,
Woven like verses, a rhythm, a rhyme.
As daylight wanes, mysteries unfold,
In twilight's glow, our hopes are bold.

Beneath the arch of an indigo dome,
We wander, we dream, we call this home.
With every sigh, a wish is spun,
In twilight's embrace, we are all one.

So let the night sing its haunting refrain,
A lullaby soft in its silvery chain.
For in the stillness, secrets reside,
Threads of twilight, where magic hides.

Tales Woven in Hues of Dusk

In hues of dusk, our tales are spun,
Echoes of laughter, the day is done.
With each brush of twilight, colors blend,
As stories unfurl, with no end.

The sky ignites in shades of fire,
Painting the world with deep desire.
Like ancient scrolls, the whispers flow,
In the heart of dusk, our secrets grow.

Each moment a fragment, a picture frame,
Chasing horizons, we build our name.
In shadows long, we find our grace,
Embracing life's dance in every space.

The twilight beckons with its gentle charm,
Revealing the magic that keeps us warm.
As stars peek out to share the night,
In hues of dusk, our dreams take flight.

Let's weave our stories with threads of gold,
Embroidering moments, both brave and bold.
For in the tapestry of nights gone by,
With tales woven, our spirits soar high.

A Tapestry Beneath Celestial Wings

Beneath celestial wings, we find our way,
In a tapestry bright, where shadows play.
Stardust gathers to hear our call,
As dreams take flight, we rise, we fall.

The cosmos sings a lullaby sweet,
Awakening hope with each heart's beat.
Galaxies swirl in a dance of light,
Guiding our spirits through the night.

With every thread, a story ignites,
Woven in whispers of myriad sights.
In the silence, we learn to embrace,
The wonders that life freely can trace.

So let us drift on starlit streams,
Explore the realm of our wildest dreams.
For beneath celestial wings, we belong,
In a tapestry woven, where we are strong.

Together we laugh, together we sigh,
In this grand design, we soar, we fly.
With hearts intertwined, forever in tune,
Beneath celestial wings, we'll always bloom.

Shadows Cast in Lavender Gleam

In lavender gleam, the shadows play,
Casting silhouettes at the end of the day.
Whispers of twilight dance on the breeze,
As night's gentle hand begins to tease.

Beneath the arches of dusky skies,
Dreams flicker softly, like fireflies.
Every heartbeat sings, a silent refrain,
In shadows cast where the magic remains.

The air is thick with the scent of peace,
As worries fade and the burdens cease.
In lavender light, we find release,
Cradled in night, our souls are at ease.

With each gentle step, we welcome the night,
Unraveling secrets bathed in twilight.
In the hush of shadows, together we stand,
In lavender gleam, we'll hold each hand.

So let us journey through whispers and dreams,
In the glow of the night, where hope redeems.
For in shadows cast, our hearts will gleam,
Together we'll weave our lavender dream.

Starlit Patterns in Whispered Tales

In the hush of night, they gleam,
Stories woven in silver streams.
Each twinkle holds a secret bright,
Guiding dreams in gentle flight.

Moonlit paths where shadows play,
Whispers float on the cool, soft sway.
Every star a fable spun,
Of journeys started, never done.

In the breeze, a tale unfolds,
Of magic nights and hearts that hold.
Patterns drawn in cosmic lace,
Binding fate in boundless space.

Glimmers of hope, in darkness deep,
Guarding wishes we dare to keep.
Dance of light upon the shore,
Where echoes linger evermore.

So let the night weave its embrace,
As dreams take flight in endless grace.
With starlit patterns guiding way,
We chase the dawn, not far away.

Threads of the Cosmos: Spun in Midnight

In the tapestry of the vast unknown,
Threads of stardust shimmer and groan.
Spun in darkness, where silence reigns,
The whispers of time weave through our veins.

Midnight's cloak wraps secrets tight,
Each thread a story born of night.
Knots of fate, both tangled and clear,
In the cosmos' heart, we hold dear.

Celestial webs, both strong and frail,
Crafting journeys on a starlit trail.
With every touch of cosmic grace,
Our spirits soar through boundless space.

Dreams are woven with golden thread,
In the quietude, our hopes are fed.
For every wish cast in the air,
Is a promise whispered, soft and rare.

Through the night, we find our place,
In the threads of the cosmos, we embrace.
So let the midnight wind softly call,
As we gather the threads that unite us all.

A Tapestry of Echoes and Woodlands

In the woodland's heart, where echoes dwell,
A tapestry of life weaves stories to tell.
Branches whispering secrets of old,
In the arms of the trees, mysteries unfold.

Moonlight dapples through leaves so fair,
Casting shadows that dance in the air.
A symphony played by nightingale's song,
In the silence of dusk, we all belong.

Each rustling leaf holds a tale untold,
Of adventures shared, both brave and bold.
With the touch of the wind, they sing in delight,
Binding the past with the soft glow of night.

The roots, they wander, beneath the ground,
Connecting the echoes that always surround.
In this tapestry, life weaves through time,
Every heartbeat a pulse, every whisper a rhyme.

So wander these woods of the woven embrace,
Where echoes and stories find their place.
In the heart of the forest, we're never alone,
For the tapestry calls us all back home.

Shadows Dance in the Weaving Light

Beneath the glow of the evening star,
Shadows gather, near and far.
They twist and twirl in the soft, warm glow,
Dancing gently to a tune we know.

In the fading light, they play their part,
Crafting stories that touch the heart.
With every flicker, every sigh,
They whisper dreams that never die.

Colors blend as day meets night,
Crafting moments, both dark and bright.
In the flickering glow, time takes flight,
As shadows dance in the weaving light.

They chase the echoes of laughter and cheer,
Weaving memories we hold dear.
Through the twilight, their tale shall soar,
In every shadow, we find something more.

So let the shadows twirl and glide,
In the maze of light, we take our stride.
For in this dance of dusk's embrace,
We find the magic that time can't erase.

Echoes Beneath the Feathered Arch

In the forest deep, where shadows play,
Whispers of magic drift and sway.
Feathered wings brush the leaves so fine,
Echoes of ancient tales intertwine.

Beneath the archway, light softly gleams,
Casting shadows where the sunlight dreams.
A flicker of hope in the dark of night,
Illuminates paths with glimmers bright.

The laughter of sprites dances on air,
As secrets are spoken with tender care.
Songs of the wild carry hearts so free,
Beneath the arch, they call to thee.

In twilight's embrace, the world holds its breath,
Life intertwines with whispers of death.
Stars twinkle softly, a celestial guide,
Leading lost souls to where dreams abide.

So linger awhile, let your spirit soar,
Among feathered arches, there's always more.
For in every echo, a story remains,
Beneath woven branches, where magic reigns.

Starlit Weavings of Gossamer Dreams

In the still of night where silence hums,
Gossamer threads from the heavens come.
Stars weave their tales in the fabric of time,
Crafting soft dreams in a cosmic rhyme.

Skies dressed in velvet, a canvas divine,
Each twinkle a secret, a sweet subtle sign.
Wishes are whispered to the moon's gentle light,
As starlit weavings unfurl in the night.

Beneath the vast vault, where shadows convene,
Fleeting moments flicker, elusive, unseen.
The heart of the dreamer, a beacon so bright,
Guides wayward spirits through the folds of night.

With every heartbeat, the cosmos will sigh,
As dreams soar on wings, and gently fly.
Tethered to stardust, they drift and glide,
In the realm of the dreamer, where magic abides.

So linger awhile, where the ether will sing,
To the rhythm of wishes and hope they bring.
For in starlit weavings, foundations are laid,
Of dreams that unfurl in silence and shade.

Impressions in Faded Velvet Hues

In corners of memory, colors will fade,
Whispers of time where dreams were laid.
Faded velvet hues in shadows entwine,
Carrying echoes of stories divine.

Each brushstroke of twilight, a gentle caress,
Painting the moments we long to possess.
Lost in the layers of what used to be,
Impressions are captured, eternally free.

From sepia whispers to pastels of light,
The palette of love dances, shining so bright.
Soft laughter rings out, as echoes of yore,
Reviving the heart, opening its door.

With every soft sigh, a connection is clear,
In faded reflections, we hold what is dear.
Days may grow distant, yet memories stay,
Impressions of velvet in soft shades of gray.

So cherish the moments, let your heart sing,
In the tapestry woven, the joy that it brings.
For in fading colors, where stories unfold,
There's beauty in memories, precious as gold.

Beneath the Gaze of the Mythic Guardian

In the shadows cast by the ancient trees,
Lurks a guardian with a watchful ease.
Eyes like lanterns, gleaming in night,
Beneath their gaze, dreams take flight.

With fur as soft as the evening mist,
Whispers of wisdom cannot be missed.
Mythic tales wrap around every paw,
Binding the forest in an unbroken law.

Beneath the stars, where magic resides,
He guides the lost on ephemeral rides.
In silence, he waits in the depths of the dark,
Serving as hope, a warm, glowing spark.

So tread lightly, dear heart, as you wander near,
For the guardian watches, his intentions clear.
With every step forward, trust your own way,
For beneath his gaze, fear fades away.

Embrace the night with its mysteries grand,
With the mythic guardian, take your stand.
For in every corner where shadows remain,
A tale is waiting, bound in the chain.

Luminescent Fabrics of Mystical Origins

In shadows where whispers weave their tale,
Threads of starlight glide, uncovering veil.
With each stitch, a secret softly glows,
A fabric of dreams where magic flows.

The tapestry hums with a silent song,
Binding the night, where shadows belong.
Patterns of hope in each delicate seam,
A world reborn in the weaver's dream.

Through twilight's embrace, colors ignite,
Luminescent fibers spark with delight.
The lore of the ancients breathes through the loom,
A dance of the cosmos, dispelling the gloom.

Beneath the soft gleam of the moon's silver kiss,
Fabrics entwine in a gossamer bliss.
Each thread tells a story, a vibrant spell,
In luminescent realms, where wonders dwell.

Threading Dreams Beneath the Celestial Gaze

Stitching the night with a needle of light,
Dreams wander freely, like stars in their flight.
Under the vastness of ever-turned skies,
A tapestry weaves where imagination flies.

Each thread holds a whisper, a wish in the dark,
Tales of adventure, from flame to a spark.
Colors cascade as the moon gently smiles,
Awakening journeys that stretch for miles.

Beneath the celestial, endless and grand,
A world finds its rhythm, a beat so well-planned.
Weaving the fabric of what could have been,
A dance in the twilight, lost dreams found again.

In patterns of hope, the heartache dissolves,
Each stitch a reminder of how it resolves.
Threading the stars till the dawn's rosy rise,
Beneath the celestial, the storyteller's prize.

Chronicles in Lavender Hues and Edges

In lavender whispers, a story unfolds,
Soft edges entwined with the magic of old.
Chronicles laced in the twilight's embrace,
Each thread a moment, a journey to trace.

Beneath azure skies where the wildflowers play,
The fabric of time softly breathes and sways.
Hues of remembrance dance through the air,
A patchwork of moments, both fragile and rare.

As twilight descends, the colors ignite,
Painting the shadows, evoking delight.
Each stitch carries whispers from ages gone by,
Chronicles woven, as memories sigh.

In lavender shifts, the heart learns to see,
The beauty in edges that set the soul free.
A story retold in the softest embrace,
Chronicles linger in time and in space.

Cosmic Lacings Underneath Fading Light

In the quiet of night, where dreams intertwine,
Cosmic lacings shimmer, all woven divine.
Underneath fading light, a mystery grows,
Fabrics of stardust, where time overflows.

Glimmers of hope paint the edges of dark,
Every twinkling star a celestial mark.
Weaving the galaxies with threads bold and bright,
Unraveling wonders that dance in the night.

As shadows retreat, and the dawn breaks anew,
The cosmic creations reshape what is true.
In soft glowing hues, each whisper takes flight,
Cosmic lacings beckon from realms out of sight.

In the fabric of dreams, connections unite,
Tales of adventure, lost in the light.
Underneath fading stars, new stories take form,
Cosmic lacings cradle the heart, keep it warm.

Whispers of Twilight Threads

In the hush where shadows play,
Softly dance the threads of grey.
Secrets echo in the night,
Woven dreams take airy flight.

Starlight twinkles, soft and bright,
Guiding hearts with gentle light.
Whispers linger, tales arcane,
In twilight's grasp, no soul in vain.

Moonbeams swirl on whispered sighs,
Chasing visions, soaring high.
Time stands still, in silence bound,
In twilight's keep, lost dreams are found.

Leaves will flutter, spirits glide,
In the dusk, where thoughts reside.
A tapestry of night and day,
With every thread, we find our way.

In the twilight's tender care,
Every heart reveals a prayer.
Embers glow in soft retreat,
As the woven stories meet.

Mysteries in the Indigo Gloom

Beneath the boughs where shadows creep,
Secrets in the garden sleep.
Indigo whispers veil the moon,
In the night, we hum a tune.

Dreams like petals strewn around,
In the hush, a mystic sound.
Shimmering pools of softest night,
Calling lost souls to take flight.

Voices echo through the trees,
Swaying softly with the breeze.
Mysterious tales wrapped in fog,
In twilight's heart, our thoughts will jog.

Glimmers pulse in corners dim,
As the stars begin to swim.
In the gloom, we trace our thoughts,
Finding solace in the knots.

Together we unlock the door,
To realms where dreams and shadows soar.
In indigo's embrace we roam,
A whispered world, our sacred home.

Tapestries Woven in Dusk's Embrace

Dusk descends, a velvet shroud,
Echoing laughter, soft and loud.
Threads of gold in twilight's blend,
Hopes and dreams begin to mend.

Every heartbeat, every sigh,
Woven tales that never die.
In the twilight, secrets bestow,
Fading light that starts to glow.

The fabric of the night unfolds,
With stories waiting to be told.
Each starlit point, a spark of fate,
In dusk's embrace, we celebrate.

Silken shadows weave and play,
Entwining paths of night and day.
In the tapestry's gentle spin,
A world emerges deep within.

Hold the threads with tender grace,
In the calm, we find our place.
Woven dreams, bright and pure,
In dusk's embrace, we will endure.

Shadows of the Celestial Loom

Stars ignite in endless dance,
As shadows shift, we steal a glance.
Celestial threads intertwine,
In the night's embrace, we shine.

Galaxies whisper ancient lore,
Of wanderers, lost on distant shores.
Every flicker, every gleam,
Weaves the fabric of a dream.

A silver thread through cosmic night,
Guides lost souls toward the light.
In the loom of fate and chance,
The universe invites our glance.

Secrets twine around our hearts,
In every shadow, magic starts.
With each sigh, in silence loom,
Celestial whispers break the gloom.

In the tapestry, we find our call,
As stars unfold their silvery thrall.
Embracing shadows, bold and bright,
We weave our dreams in endless night.

The Griffin's Mane of Cosmic Weavings

In the depths where shadows sway,
A griffin rides the milky way.
Its mane a blaze of woven stars,
With secrets whispered from afar.

Through cosmic threads it weaves its tale,
On stardust trails, it will not fail.
Majestic wings in twilight's glow,
A guardian of what lies below.

Each feather gleams with ancient lore,
Its roar like thunder, legends soar.
In midnight's cradle, dreams ignite,
As hearts alight with pure delight.

From constellations, magic spills,
The griffin knows the world's vast thrills.
In wonders spun from night's embrace,
It guides the lost to safer space.

So when the stars begin to dance,
Look up with hope, partake the chance.
For in the heavens, fierce yet tame,
You'll find the griffin's cosmic flame.

Whimsies Wrapped in Night's Caress

In quiet nooks of shadowed air,
Whimsical dreams begin to flare.
Wrapped in night's soft, silken veil,
They weave through stars, a tender trail.

Moonbeams twirl like dancers bright,
Each twinkling spark a pure delight.
Gentle sighs in the velvet black,
As laughter echoes, never lack.

In corners where the shadows play,
Whimsies flutter, drift, and sway.
They paint the world in shades of gleam,
And wrap our hearts in silent dream.

With every whisper, night will sing,
Of secret paths and hidden things.
They pirouette with grace and ease,
A lullaby upon the breeze.

So close your eyes and dream anew,
Let night enfold, a softer hue.
For whimsies wrapped in moonlit trance,
Awaken hope, give life a chance.

A Canvas of Stardust and Shadow

Upon the night, a canvas sprawls,
With stardust scattered, shadow calls.
Each point of light a story spun,
In twilight's breath, creation's fun.

A brush of fate with colors rare,
Each hue a promise, light to share.
In ink of dreams, the silence hums,
As whispers rise, the heart succumbs.

Sketching hopes in constellations,
A tapestry of aspirations.
With every stroke, a wish unfurls,
In cosmic dance, the magic swirls.

So paint your dreams upon the night,
With every twinkle, find your light.
For on this canvas, bold and wide,
The universe holds you deep inside.

Embrace the shadows, light the flame,
In stardust's glow, speak your name.
For in this canvas, vast and free,
Your spirit sings in harmony.

Tapestries of Silence Beneath the Moon

Beneath the moon's soft, watchful gaze,
Tapestries of silence blaze.
In whispers woven, night unfolds,
Ancient secrets softly told.

Each thread a sigh, each color calm,
A healing peace, a tranquil balm.
In shadowed light where spirits play,
The heart finds rest at the end of day.

The stars like stitches, bright and neat,
Sew together dreams, bittersweet.
While night's embrace holds tight the fears,
A tapestry of silent tears.

In midnight's hush, all worries fade,
As peace encircles, serenely laid.
The moonlight bathes the earth in grace,
A tranquil touch, a warm embrace.

So wander through the quiet night,
And let the stars be your guiding light.
For in the silence beneath the moon,
Your spirit finds its perfect tune.

Celestial Patterns in Fading Light

Stars shimmer softly, twinkling bright,
Beneath the veil of encroaching night.
Whispers of the cosmos, calm and clear,
Drawn in the dance of the atmosphere.

Galaxies swirl in a vast embrace,
Painting the skies with a timeless grace.
Echoes of ancient tales take flight,
In the canvas of fading, gentle light.

Constellations tell of journeys grand,
Mapping the dreams of a weary land.
Each flicker a story, lost yet near,
In the tapestry woven with hope and fear.

Moonbeams cascade, like silver threads,
Illuminating what the darkness dreads.
A symphony whispered, soft and low,
Guiding the heart where the wanderers go.

In this twilight, wisdom calls their names,
While the night unveils its shimmering games.
Celestial patterns, forever bright,
In the depths of our souls, a soothing light.

Whispers of the Past in Threaded Shadows

In the quiet of dusk, shadows entwine,
Whispers of stories, ancient and divine.
Threaded through time, a delicate lace,
Echoes of laughter fill the empty space.

Moonlight drapes softly over the ground,
Hushed secrets linger, waiting to be found.
The breeze carries tales of yore,
Bridging the gap to what came before.

Flickering lanterns dance on the walls,
Casting soft images as twilight falls.
Every corner holds a memory's glow,
A tapestry woven, whispering low.

Hidden in pathways, footfalls may rest,
Dreams and regrets are intricately pressed.
In the shadows, a story still sits,
Waiting for hearts where the past still fits.

From rafters above, the echoes will sigh,
Threads of remembrance never may die.
In the silence, the past comes alive,
In the whispers of time, the spirits thrive.

Stories in the Weaving of Cosmic Light

In the loom of the heavens, stars brightly glow,
Weaving their stories in the night's gentle flow.
Galaxies twirl in a waltz so sweet,
Every thread in the fabric, a heartbeat.

Nebulae blossom, like dreams on the rise,
Painting the canvas of infinite skies.
Planets once silent now sing in delight,
With tales intertwined in celestial light.

A comet races, reflecting the past,
Ancient prophecies woven to last.
In the tapestry grand, secrets reside,
Stories of wonders and worlds yet untied.

Starlight champions the quest of the night,
Illuminating paths to futures so bright.
Each pinprick a whisper, a promise to keep,
In the cosmic embrace, the dreams softly leap.

From the shadows of time, voices will rise,
Narratives swirling like fireflies.
In the weaving of light, we learn to unite,
Creating our stories in the depths of the night.

Tones and Textures Beneath the Aerie

Beneath the great aeon, where echoes abide,
Tones of the earth in soft whispers slide.
Textures of nature weave tales through the air,
A symphony painted with utmost care.

Crisp leaves awaken to the dawn's embrace,
Rustling their secrets with delicate grace.
The heart of the forest, a poetic song,
Calls to the wanderers, inviting them long.

Mountains in whispers, stoic and true,
Stand guard over rivers that sparkle like dew.
The colors of life from the roots to the sky,
Immerse in a palette where dreams learn to fly.

In valleys forgotten, a promise unspooled,
Where shadows and sunlight have lovingly pooled.
Tones blend harmoniously, crafting a tale,
Of journeys and longings that never grow stale.

Here in the stillness, the spirit will soar,
Amidst the vibrations, forever we explore.
Beneath the great aeon, where echoes abide,
Tones and textures weave tales that won't hide.

Ethereal Patterns in the Loom of Reality

In twilight's embrace, shadows weave,
Threads of whispers that never leave.
Through glimmers of hope, the heart shall soar,
In life's great tapestry, we seek for more.

Each stitch of fate, so finely spun,
Holds tales of laughter, of loss, of fun.
As stars align in the great unknown,
We dance to the rhythm of dreams we've grown.

Mysterious knots tie past and present,
In vibrant hues, our hearts are crescent.
With every heartbeat, a story unfolds,
Enigma hidden in soft, silken folds.

The loom of time, both fierce and gentle,
Crafts the patterns, the joys and the mental.
In nooks of wonder, we find the thread,
Illuminating pathways where few have tread.

Beyond the veil, where shadows flit,
The tapestry weaves, we quietly sit.
In ethereal realms, we craft our bliss,
A legacy spun from moments, with a kiss.

Starlit Stories in the Fabric of Flight

Upon wings of night, the stars allow,
A journey of dreams, in silence we vow.
Each twinkle, a tale of ages gone by,
In starlit stories, our hopes learn to fly.

The fabric of flight wraps all in delight,
With feathers of courage, we chase the light.
Through ethereal skies, where wishes take wing,
In midnight's embrace, our spirits will sing.

Galaxies bloom, like flowers in space,
Every heartbeat, a rhythm, a trace.
With tales of the cosmos, our spirits unite,
In starlit whispers, we find our true sight.

The constellations, they guide us with care,
A map of the heart, a promise to share.
In luminous threads, our destinies weave,
As night wraps around, we learn to believe.

With each fleeting moment, the magic ignites,
In dreams interwoven, our hearts take to heights.
In the embrace of the heavens, we soar high,
Starlit stories in the fabric of sky.

Interwoven Dreams of Fantasy and Lore

In realms where the wildest dreams aspire,
Interwoven threads of fantasy inspire.
The echoes of magic, where fairies play,
In whispered enchantments, we find our way.

With dragons in flight and castles that gleam,
Each moment a spark, igniting the dream.
Threads of old legends beneath our feet,
In the heart of the forest, our fates shall meet.

From whispers of giants to sprites in bloom,
We dance in the magic, dispelling the gloom.
With tales spun in starlight, forever we roam,
In the tapestry woven, we find our true home.

Every heart carries a tale yet untold,
In the fabric of fantasy, together we hold.
As myths come alive on this mythical shore,
In the interwoven dreams, we're forever more.

With every embrace of the moon's gentle glow,
The lore of our spirits begins to bestow.
Together we dance in the light of our lore,
Interwoven dreams forever explore.

The Last Threads of Daylight Retold

As daylight wanes, the sky turns gold,
The last threads of time, in whispers bold.
With every sunset, a promise is spun,
In the twilight's embrace, a day is won.

Shadows stretch long, dancing in light,
The whispers of evening awaken the night.
With colors that fade, new dreams take their cue,
In the fabric of endings, beginnings shine through.

The canvas of dusk, where stories reside,
In this quiet magic, our hearts open wide.
Each moment a stitch in the tapestry rare,
In the last threads of daylight, we breathe the air.

With echoes of laughter, we capture the scene,
In the whispers of twilight, our spirits convene.
As memories linger in soft, muted glow,
The last threads of daylight gently flow.

Together we stand, as the stars start to peep,
In the dusk's tender grasp, our secrets we keep.
Every sunset, a chapter, a tale left to unfold,
The last threads of daylight, forever retold.

A Tapestry of Secrets and Stars

In twilight's embrace, whispers sigh,
Secrets woven where shadows lie.
Threads of starlight weave and twine,
A tapestry rich, of fate divine.

Moonlit strands in the gentle night,
Hearts entwined, dreams take flight.
With each stitch, a story unfolds,
Ancient tales in the fabric told.

Beneath the whispers of the trees,
The fabric dances with the breeze.
Every color a memory framed,
In this realm where hope is named.

Hidden gems in the quiet dark,
Luminous threads that leave their mark.
In every shadow, a secret stays,
Painting the world in mysterious ways.

A tapestry spun in the night air,
With dreams and wishes woven with care.
Caught in the weave of time's embrace,
In the heart of magic, we find our place.

Guardians Beneath the Starlit Sky

In the hush of night, they softly tread,
Guardians awake, where dreams are spread.
Wings of twilight, they gently soar,
Beneath the stars, forevermore.

Voices of old in the midnight air,
Binding the lost with tender care.
Each spark a light, glimmering bright,
A promise kept in the silent night.

Around the fire, stories ignite,
Of worlds unseen, beyond our sight.
With hearts aglow, they stand as one,
Protecting dreams till the morning sun.

Whispers of magic in every sigh,
Guardians called from the starlit high.
Each twinkle a vow, a guardian's plea,
To shield the hopes of you and me.

In shadows deep, their watchful gaze,
Through silent nights and sunlit days.
Embraced by stars, where shadows die,
Guardians dwell beneath the sky.

Interludes of Fantasy and Shadow

In realms where echoes find their way,
Interludes bloom, both night and day.
A whisper here, a shadow there,
Magic dances on the air.

With moonlight's touch, the dreams entwine,
Fantasy weaves through the divine.
Colors collide as shadows play,
In a tapestry of night and day.

Stories linger in the dusky light,
Painting the world in shades of white.
Each breath a note in a timeless song,
Where the hearts of dreamers all belong.

In every glance, a tale awaits,
Intermingled with fate's threads and mates.
As time flows gently, our dreams align,
In fantasy's arms, our spirits shine.

A world unfolds in a whispered tone,
Interludes spark in hearts we've grown.
Together we'll wander through shadow and light,
In realms of fantasy, taking flight.

Dreamscapes of Myth and Thread

In dreamscapes vast, where legends dwell,
Myths are born, like a hidden spell.
Threads of wonder stitch the night,
Creating visions, sculpting light.

With every heartbeat, a tale unfolds,
Of heroes bold and treasures gold.
Through the fabric of dreams, we roam,
In enchanted lands, we find our home.

Sylvan woods and mountains high,
Where echoes of laughter never die.
With every whisper, myths are spun,
In the tapestry woven, we become one.

Moonbeams guide with silken touch,
Unraveling threads that mean so much.
In these dreamscapes, we take flight,
Exploring realms beyond the night.

With each tread on this hallowed ground,
The essence of magic is ever found.
In every smile, in every thread,
The fabric of myth is gently spread.

Silks of Secrets in the Plains of Dusk

In twilight's embrace, whispers weave soft,
Threads of shadows dance, rising aloft.
Silks of secrets call, beneath a pale moon,
As stars twinkle gently, a delicate tune.

Winds carry tales of fields long forgotten,
Where lovers once trysted, and dreams were begotten.
The horizon blurs, colors intertwine,
As dusk wraps the world in a shimmering line.

Crickets sing low, in harmony's grace,
Expectant sighs fill the tranquil space.
A spellbinding hush blankets the land,
While magic unseen flows like golden sand.

Echoes of laughter float softly on air,
In the realm of the night, beyond all despair.
The fabric of time gently unfolds,
Weaving fables of hearts, both daring and bold.

With each silky thread, a story is spun,
In twilight's warm glow, new journeys begun.
Secrets entwine in the planes of dusk,
Where wishes take flight, in the twilight's husk.

Fiber Mosaics Beneath the Watchful Eye

Beneath a vast sky, a canvas is laid,
Fiber mosaics, where dreams are portrayed.
Every stitch whispers, in colors so bright,
Stories of beings that dance in the light.

The watchful eye glimmers, guarding the night,
A realm full of wonders, both fragile and light.
With threads of the past, the present, the now,
In the loom of existence, the magic we plow.

In gardens of hope, where the wildflowers bloom,
Life's tapestries flourish, dispelling the gloom.
Each woven fragment, a charm to behold,
With secrets and stories intricately told.

The fibers entwined, in passion's embrace,
Beneath the watchful eye, we find our own place.
Patterns of magic weave through each beat,
In this mystical realm, our hearts find their feat.

Every moment a thread, each breath a new stitch,
Fabric of life, so vivid, so rich.
Together we soar, with wings made of dreams,
In the fiber mosaics, where wonder redeems.

Twilight Weavings in Dreamers' Glade

In Dreamers' glade, where shadows blend,
Twilight weavings stretch, never to end.
Whispers of magic, like soft velvet night,
In every corner, sweet echoes of light.

Breezes carry wishes, lands far and near,
A symphony stirs, sweet melody clear.
Woven together, hopes dance in the breeze,
In a twilight embrace, as time gently flees.

Starlit threads twinkle, so wondrously bright,
Patterns of dreams in the fabric of night.
A tapestry chronicling moments sublime,
Where hearts interlace, transcending all time.

The glow of the moon bathes the world in gold,
As stories of ages quietly unfold.
Each breath, a color, each sigh, a refrain,
In the weavings of twilight, love knows no pain.

With each fleeting hour, fresh wonders arise,
In the glade of dreamers, beneath sprawling skies.
Together we linger, in magic, we write,
In twilight's embrace, forever in flight.

Threads of the Mysterious Celestial World

In the mysterious realms where starlight is spun,
Threads of creation glitter, all woven as one.
Each galaxy pulses, a heartbeat of dreams,
In the tapestry cosmic, where wonder redeems.

Planets entwined in a delicate dance,
A ballad of ages, of chance and romance.
With colors unfathomed, they swirl and they blend,
In the fabric of night, where horizons extend.

Sewing the heavens with gossamer strands,
Painting the cosmos with luminous hands.
Destinies twinkle in the depths of the void,
Threads of the universe, forever deployed.

Every comet that streaks, every meteor's flight,
Tells tales of the cosmos, so vivid, so bright.
In this celestial world, a grand story's spun,
Where dreams meet the starlight, and hearts beat as one.

In the silent embrace of twilight's soft breath,
We dance with the stars, defying all depth.
Threads of the mysterious, forever entwined,
In the universe vast, our essence aligned.

Celestial Stitches Weaving Through the Night

In the vault of the starry dome,
Threads of silver weave and roam.
Stitch by stitch, the heavens sigh,
Calling dreams from dusk's deep sky.

Moonlight dances on twilight's loom,
Filling the world with whispered bloom.
Each twinkle, a secret softly spun,
In the tapestry where night begun.

Constellations, a map of lore,
Guide the lost to a distant shore.
With every seam, a story's told,
Of brave hearts and spirits bold.

Through the fabric of shadows they glide,
Stars like sentinels at our side.
Their glow, a compass for the soul,
Binding time, makes the wanderer whole.

So stitch your hopes in the fabric bright,
Let them soar on wings of night.
For in every thread, there is a light,
Celestial whispers keep dreams in sight.

Woven Whispers in the Gale of Twilight

In twilight's hush, the breezes weave,
Secrets held, as hearts believe.
With every sigh, the shadows play,
Whispering tales that drift away.

Leaves rustle softly, a gentle song,
Entwining dreams where they belong.
The world is cloaked in twilight's spell,
While winds carry stories none can tell.

Echoes of laughter in the dimming light,
Stars awaken, softly bright.
Through the dusk, the magic flows,
Woven whispers in twilight's close.

Beneath the trees, the spirits dance,
In delicate steps of old romance.
Every flicker, a magic chance,
Weaving wonder in life's expanse.

As shadows gather, secrets are spun,
In the calm of night when day is done.
Listen closely, the gales recite,
Woven whispers in the fading light.

Chronicles of the Heart in Subtle Threads

In the fabric where emotions dwell,
Heartstrings play their silent spell.
Each pulse a chapter, raw and true,
Chronicles spun in shades of blue.

Love's tender stitch, a fleeting grace,
Woven softly in time and space.
Every tear, a silver seam,
Sewing together the frayed and dreamt.

In hallowed beams of softest gold,
Stories linger, waiting to be told.
Through laughter's echo and sorrow's thread,
The heart's deep narrative is gently fed.

Silent moments, fierce and bold,
In the loom of life, we weave the old.
With every heartbeat, we craft anew,
A tapestry rich in every hue.

So gather your threads, embrace your art,
For each woven tale is a work of heart.
In the chronicles that time extends,
Subtle threads bind, as the journey bends.

Echoing Colors of the Mysterious Night

In the night where shadows teem,
Colors whisper, woven dreams.
Midnight blue and emerald glows,
Tell of secrets only night knows.

The stars paint pictures in the dark,
While fireflies flicker, a glowing spark.
Each hue a tale, elusive, light,
Echoing colors of the silent night.

Violet whispers ride on the breeze,
Carrying stories through ancient trees.
With every rustle, the night unfolds,
Mysteries wrapped in hues untold.

Underneath the silver moon,
Colors swirl in a vibrant tune.
Where dreams and shadows softly meet,
Life's rich palette forms beneath our feet.

So walk with wonder, let colors guide,
In the mysteries where we abide.
For in the night's enchanting flight,
Echoing colors dance, reveal the light.

Flights of Fancy Beneath Starry Skies

Beneath the shimmer of a thousand stars,
Dreamers wander where the magic lies.
Whispers float on the silver breeze,
As night enfolds with its gentle sighs.

Wings of wonder, they take to flight,
Painting tales on the canvas bright.
In every heart, a flicker glows,
A promise kept in the velvet night.

Luminous trails danced across the dark,
Each flicker promising new life anew.
In shadows deep, soft laughter sung,
Guided by dreams and starlit dew.

With every breath, horizons shift,
Casting spells, enchantments weave.
And in the heart of every dreamer,
A world awakes, primed to believe.

In boundless realms where wishes soar,
Bound by nothing, they dare to roam.
For within the night, dreams intertwine,
Creating magic, calling them home.

Enchanted Fibers in a Mystic Realm

In a grove where shadows softly play,
Threads of time spin tales untold.
Where whispers of trees hold secrets deep,
And night wraps all in its gentle fold.

Silken strands of the moon's silver touch,
Weave the dreams of a world unseen.
With every stitch, the fabric hums,
A tapestry rich, where spirits convene.

Crimson blooms and emerald leaves,
Draped in wonder, a vibrant sight.
Looms of fate, in the twilight spun,
Knit together the day and night.

In corners where the fairies dance,
Glowing embers light up the dark.
Every soul seeks a place to dream,
A sanctuary, a gleaming spark.

Together woven in a cosmic scheme,
These fibers twine in the heart of all.
Embrace the magic, and let it flow,
For in this realm, we hear the call.

Stitched Memories of a Dusk-Kissed Night

As day concedes to the evening's hush,
A quilt of colors blankets the sky.
Every stitch tells a story spun,
Of love and laughter, of lows and high.

Memories twinkling like distant stars,
Each glimmer holds fragments of time.
On woven threads, the tales we share,
Life's patchwork made sublime.

In twilight's glow, forgotten dreams rise,
Carried softly on the night's embrace.
Echoes of laughter, whispers of hope,
A tender touch in this sacred space.

Beneath the blanket of a dusky hue,
Hearts unite, stitching fate's design.
Every moment, a thread that binds,
Tales of life in the stars align.

So gather 'round this shimmering cloth,
Embrace the warmth of the night's delight.
For in each fold, a memory sleeps,
Glimmers softly in the fading light.

Palette of the Otherworldly Dawn

In the hush where twilight meets allure,
A palette blooms, enchanting and bright.
The canvas swirls with colors untold,
Awakening magic in the morning light.

Brushstrokes of amber and blush collide,
As daybreak heralds a wondrous sight.
Whispers of dawn weave through the trees,
Inviting all to bask in its light.

From sapphire skies to golden fields,
Nature paints with a lover's touch.
Every hue a story spun,
In the morning's glow, we find so much.

As the sun rises, shadows retreat,
Revealing dreams set free to roam.
In every petal, in every sigh,
The essence of magic spills through the loam.

So cherish the dawn where colors dance,
In this fleeting moment, let spirits soar.
For in the heart of each otherworldly morn,
Lies an invitation to dream forevermore.

Mysteries Spun in Ethereal Fabrics

In a realm where whispers dance,
Threads of silver weave a chance.
Secrets hidden from our sight,
Sparkling softly in the night.

Stars above in silent flight,
Knitting dreams with pure delight.
Every stitch a tale unfolds,
In the loom where fate beholds.

Winds of fate do gently blow,
Carrying stories lost in glow.
Ethereal fabrics wrap us tight,
Guiding us through darkest night.

Colors vibrant, shadows cast,
Echoing memories from the past.
Each thread tells of love and loss,
Binding us, no matter the cost.

From the loom, the weaver sways,
Crafting magic in mystic ways.
With a flick, a twist, a turn,
In the heart, the embers burn.

Stories from the Loom of Dreams

Once upon a midnight clear,
Dreams arise without a fear.
Looms of fate begin their hum,
Whispering tales yet to come.

Threads of longing, threads of hope,
Weaving patterns, learning to cope.
Each tale spun from laughter sighs,
Beneath the vast and starry skies.

In the tapestry of the night,
Every color catches light.
Stories bloom from darkened seams,
Rippling through the land of dreams.

Past the shadows, voices call,
Echoes of the great and small.
From the loom, we weave our fates,
In the silence, love awaits.

Magic flows through warp and weft,
In the silence, treasures left.
Every dream a thread divine,
In a universe of time.

Echoes of Twilight in Tattered Threads

In twilight's glow, the whispers start,
Tattered threads that pull the heart.
Shadows dance in soft embrace,
Echoes softly leave their trace.

Stars emerge like distant sighs,
Fading in the velvet skies.
Each patch tells of struggles fought,
In the fabric, lessons taught.

Memories cradled in the seams,
Woven deep within our dreams.
Fragments lost but never gone,
They linger on, they carry on.

The weaver's hand, both firm and slight,
Spins the stories of the night.
In every knot, a mystery grows,
In every fold, a spirit glows.

Beneath the moon's enchanted gaze,
Time unwinds in endless ways.
Tattered threads still hold their place,
In the tapestry of grace.

The Secret Weave of Shadowed Heights

High above where shadows play,
The secret weave holds night at bay.
Whispers flutter, secrets gleam,
In the fabric of a dream.

Mountains rise in silent pride,
Guarding tales that time won't hide.
Threads of bravery, stitched with care,
Knotting hopes into the air.

In the silence, echoes bloom,
Filling every shadowed room.
Weaving light where darkness dwells,
In the heart, a story swells.

From the heights, the stars look down,
Kissing earth with silver crown.
Every thread a journey made,
In the loom where dreams cascade.

The weaver listens to the night,
Crafting magic, pure delight.
In secret heights, we find our voice,
In woven dreams, we all rejoice.

Flickers of Light through Woven Threads

In twilight's embrace, shadows dance,
Threads of silver, a fleeting chance.
Whispers of magic, softly tread,
Binding the worlds where dreams are bred.

Loom of fate, with delicate hands,
Weaving tales from ancient sands.
Each flicker a star, a story told,
In fabric of night, the brave and bold.

Patterns emerge in silken sway,
Guiding lost hearts along the way.
Through woven paths, together we find,
The light of truth, beautifully blind.

Cascades of color, a vibrant flight,
Illuminating secrets, pure delight.
In tapestry's warmth, we seek our place,
As time bends softly in this embrace.

In flickers of light that gently gleam,
Woven threads hold the essence of dream.
Holding us close until dawn's first light,
A dance of shadows, forever bright.

Dreamscapes Spun from Starry Looms

In the hush of night, dreams take flight,
Spun from the stars, igniting delight.
With echoes of wonder, softly they weave,
In realms of the sleeping, we dare to believe.

A canvas of velvet, adorned with bright hues,
Whispers of stories, the heart can't refuse.
Looming adventures through uncharted skies,
Where each twinkle holds promise, where magic lies.

Rivers of silver, flowing with grace,
Carrying wishes to a shimmering place.
On stardust paths where our hopes intertwine,
We breathe in the cosmos, a dream so divine.

Threads of the universe, woven so fine,
Dance in the darkness, like aged fine wine.
With each careful stitch, our spirits ignite,
Dreamscapes unfurl in the stillness of night.

In the heart of the cosmos, we wander and roam,
Finding our voices, crafting a home.
For every lost dream, a new star will bloom,
In the vastness of night, our fates resume.

Hues of Dusk in an Artist's Reverie

In shadows cast by the setting sun,
Each hue of dusk whispers, "We've begun."
On canvas of twilight, colors collide,
An artist's heart swells, no need to hide.

The brush, like a wand, dances with ease,
Capturing silence, the rustling trees.
With every stroke, a story is born,
In the twilight's glow, new worlds are sworn.

Burnt sienna spills on the edge of night,
While lavender sighs, embracing the light.
In this gentle pause, inspiration flows,
As dusk wraps around, and creativity grows.

A tapestry woven with colors rich,
Each layer a secret, a glimmering stitch.
In the quiet of dusk, the muse joins the fray,
Through the painter's eye, night turns to day.

So let us linger in this painter's trance,
As hues of dusk weave their vibrant dance.
For every brushstroke is a wish from the heart,
In an artist's reverie, we each play a part.

Patterns of the Cosmos on a Quiet Canvas

On this tranquil stretch of evening's veil,
Patterns emerge as the stars set sail.
In the hush of the night, secrets unfold,
Spinning stories of ages, both bold and old.

Constellations whisper in twinkling tones,
Each light a heartbeat, not one stands alone.
Fingers trace paths in the dark's embrace,
Mapping the cosmos, a stellar race.

A canvas of night, where dreams intertwine,
In the web of existence, a design so fine.
Galaxies swirl in a delicate dance,
Inviting our spirits to take a chance.

With every starlit blink, a tale will arise,
Unraveling truths from the vast midnight skies.
In quiet reflection, we sit side by side,
Finding our place in the dark's gentle tide.

So let the patterns guide our weary hearts,
In the quiet of night, where existence starts.
Each dream, a stitch in the universe wide,
On this canvas of stars, where wonders abide.

Celestial Threads and Oceanic Dreams

In twilight's embrace, stars softly gleam,
Waves whisper secrets, lost in a dream.
Each glimmering thread, a tale to unfold,
In the depths of the ocean, both ancient and bold.

Moonlit horizons, where skies kiss the sea,
Every ripple dances, wild and free.
With colors that shimmer, and shadows that play,
The universe beckons, guiding our way.

The currents may shift, yet treasures remain,
In the hearts of the dreamers who crave the arcane.
With eyes like the cosmos, we wander the night,
Falling through stardust, a magical flight.

So weave a fine tapestry, bright and profound,
With threads from the heavens and echoes of sound.
In the weave of existence, our stories intertwine,
In celestial threads, through space and through time.

Threads of Gold in Cosmic Realms

In the depths of the cosmos, threads shimmer and glow,
Each golden filament tells of a journey we know.
Bound by the starlight, our destinies meet,
In the vastness of time, where the echoes repeat.

With whispers of twilight, the universe sings,
Of timeless connections, the joy that it brings.
Like spinning of galaxies, distant yet near,
Threads of gold sparkle, inviting us here.

In the fabric of night, where dreams fill the air,
We gather the stardust, our wishes laid bare.
Through cosmic horizons, we travel and roam,
In the threads of existence, we find our true home.

With fingers entwined, we weave stories bright,
Of love and adventure, igniting the night.
In the tapestry woven from laughter and tears,
Threads of gold shimmer, transcending all years.

Ethereal Stitches of a Lingering Heart

Beneath the night sky, where the shadows entwine,
Ethereal stitches connect yours to mine.
Each breath is a promise, a whispered embrace,
In the fabric of time, we find our true place.

In moments of silence, our secrets we share,
The threads of our spirits are woven with care.
With every heartbeat, the distance grows small,
In the depths of our souls, we answer the call.

Though miles may divide us, we're never apart,
For love is the needle that mends every heart.
Through the tapestry woven of memories bright,
Our ethereal stitches hold fast through the night.

With colors and textures, a blend so divine,
In the loom of our lives, your heart is in mine.
As the stars bear witness to tales we impart,
Ethereal stitches bind each longing heart.

Isolated Colors of Celestial Lore

In the canvas of night, isolated hues,
Celestial lore whispers of stories and news.
In bursts of bright colors, the cosmos will gleam,
As we journey through skies, chasing every dream.

With voices of stardust, the planets will share,
Their secrets and wonders, beyond earthly care.
Each shade tells a tale, both mystical and wise,
A tapestry woven from the fabric of skies.

In twilight's soft hues, we wander alone,
Yet the colors unite us, pulling us home.
Through cycles of moons, and the sun's warm embrace,
Isolated colors find beauty in space.

So let your heart soar on the wings of the night,
Embrace every shadow, every shimmering light.
In the palette of dreams, where the stars float and soar,
We discover our place in celestial lore.

Fabric of Whimsy Under Twilight's Veil

In the hush of dusk, when shadows dance,
Threads of laughter twirl in chance.
Whispers of dreams in the fading light,
Caress the heart, and take their flight.

With every stitch, a secret spun,
Moonlight beckons, the day is done.
Colors blend in a painter's grace,
Magic lingers in this sacred space.

Time bends softly, a gentle sigh,
Stars awaken, flicker in the sky.
Each moment woven in tender care,
A tapestry rich with joy to share.

Here in twilight, where wishes gleam,
Hope dances lightly, like a dream.
The fabric of whimsy, a vibrant thread,
Wraps the night in stories unsaid.

Silken Dreams on the Edge of Night

As twilight whispers, the world transforms,
Float away on silken norms.
Dreams unfurl, a delicate lace,
Painting night in a soft embrace.

Glimmers of starlight, a wondrous show,
Twinkling secrets that ebb and flow.
In the quiet, where shadows lay,
Hope ignites, to light the way.

With every heartbeat, the magic blooms,
In private gardens, where silence looms.
Savor the stillness, the night's sweet song,
For here, dear soul, is where you belong.

Each silken thread, a dream we weave,
In the night's embrace, we dare believe.
Hold on to starlight, let wishes soar,
For night's gentle magic opens the door.

Woven Wishes in the Twilight Garden

In the twilight garden where dreams reside,
Woven wishes flourish and glide.
Petals shimmer with stories told,
In hues of wonder, a sight to behold.

Under a canopy of starlit beams,
Time unravels into enchanting schemes.
Kisses of breeze, fragrant and sweet,
Guide us softly on softest feet.

Each whispered wish, a delicate bloom,
Twirling in rhythm, dispelling gloom.
With every sigh, the magic grows,
In this secret place, love surely flows.

Nature paints canvases rich and bright,
Filling the air with sparkles of light.
In the twilight garden, we shall find,
A tapestry woven with hearts intertwined.

Threads of Enchantment

In the stillness, threads softly weave,
Enchantments born for those who believe.
In moonlit chambers where shadows play,
Stories awaken and drift away.

With each soft whisper, the night conceals,
Mysteries woven in silken reels.
The heart stirs gently at twilight's call,
Capturing moments, no fear of fall.

Glimmers of magic in every seam,
Dancing softly, like a fleeting dream.
Threads of laughter, threads of grace,
Create a sanctuary, a sacred space.

Entwined in wonders, we swing and sway,
On the delicate threads of this ballet.
Embrace the night, let the story unfold,
For in every stitch, a treasure foretold.

Night's Embrace

When the night falls and shadows creep,
In dreams, we wander, through silence deep.
Every star whispers a tale divine,
Lost in the embrace of the night's design.

The moon sings softly, a lullaby sweet,
Guiding our souls on feathered feet.
Cloaked in mystery, the dark enfolds,
Every heartbeat a story told.

Wrapped in the warmth of night's gentle arms,
We chase the echoes of hidden charms.
In this sacred stillness, we find our way,
Embracing the magic that night holds sway.

With every breath, let your worries cease,
In the night's embrace, discover your peace.
For here lies a journey, an endless flight,
In the arms of the ever-loving night.

Labyrinths of Lavender Whispers

In gardens where the shadows dance,
The lavender sways, a secret chance.
Whispers wrap around the breeze,
Carrying tales from ancient trees.

A hidden path, a winding thread,
Paths to places where dreams are bred.
In twilight's hue, the magic stirs,
As night descends, the heart concurs.

Each petal holds a gentle sigh,
As stars above begin to fly.
The echoes weave through fragrant air,
A labyrinth found, beyond compare.

Secrets Entwined in Moonlit Fibers

Beneath the glow of silvery light,
Fibers shimmer, woven tight.
Threads of stories softly glow,
In shadows deep, where secrets flow.

Each stitch a word, each knot a dream,
Entwined together, a mystic seam.
The night reveals what daylight hides,
Within the fabric, magic abides.

Through endless weaves, a tale unfolds,
Of destinies that night beholds.
In whispers soft, the truth ignites,
As moonlight stamps the dark with lights.

Beneath the Serpent's Gaze

In shadows cast by emerald scales,
A serpent watching, patience prevails.
Beneath its gaze, the whispers creep,
Of ancient foes and secrets deep.

It coils around the roots of time,
In harmony with fate's own rhyme.
A silent sentinel of lore,
Guarding paths to the unknown door.

Through twilight realms, where shadows blend,
The serpent's gaze will not suspend.
Each flicker of its watchful eyes,
Guides lost souls to their true skies.

Tangles of Celestial Color

In skies adorned with vibrant hues,
Stars spin tales, once lost to snooze.
Cosmic threads of destiny weave,
In tangled patterns, hearts believe.

A canvas where the dreams take flight,
With colors dancing in the night.
The universe sings a timeless song,
Inviting all to join along.

Beyond the reach of earthly care,
The tangled paths of stars lay bare.
In every twinkle, a wish does curl,
A cosmic dance that swirls and twirls.

Elysian Patterns of Dreams Unraveled

In whispering winds where secrets lie,
The dreams cascade like stars up high.
Each thread unwoven holds a tale,
Of distant realms where spirits sail.

Through twilight's veil, the shadows creep,
In labyrinths where lost dreams sleep.
Colors of hope in twilight blend,
In this tapestry, all worlds ascend.

Beneath a sky of azure grace,
The patterns dance in a cosmic space.
Elysian realms await their seams,
Entwined in the fabric of our dreams.

With every stitch, a wish is made,
In silken threads where magic's laid.
The essence of love and loss entwined,
A labyrinth of wonders undefined.

So let us wander through the night,
Where dreams and patterns spark delight.
Each heart's desire, a story spun,
In twilight shadows, we become one.

A Symphony of Shadows in Extravagant Threads

In the hush of night, shadows sway,
Entwined in a symphonic ballet.
The moonlit glow, a lantern bright,
Illuminates truths hidden from sight.

With every note, a spell is cast,
Echoes of time, a journey vast.
Extravagant threads of night unfurl,
As witching whispers begin to twirl.

In clandestine corners, stories dwell,
Where magic weaves a mystic spell.
Each breath of air, a sigh sublime,
Beneath the ebb and flow of time.

Within the tapestry of fears untold,
The symphony wraps its arms so bold.
A dance of dreams, a haunting art,
That stirs and tugs at the heart.

So let us sway to this shadowed tune,
Bound in the silence of the moon.
For in this night, we find our thread,
A symphony of shadows, softly spread.

Wonders Woven in Hues of Cosmic Dusk

In twilight's grasp, where wonders gleam,
The sky unveils a vivid dream.
Hues of purple, blue, and gold,
In canvas realms, new tales unfold.

Each stroke of dusk, a mystery spun,
As day concedes to night begun.
Woven whispers in the air,
Summon the magic, we long to share.

From starry depths to ocean's sigh,
The fabric breathes, and wonders cry.
A spectrum vast, beyond our gaze,
Where dreams ignite in cosmic blaze.

In the cradle of the endless skies,
Every glance reveals a prize.
A journey through these woven hues,
A tapestry where hope renews.

So linger here where shadows dance,
In cosmic dusk's enchanted trance.
For in this realm of vibrant flow,
The wonders of the universe grow.

Fabrics of Myth Beneath the Starlit Canopy

Underneath the starlit dome,
Fabrics of myth create our home.
Each twinkling light, a tale divine,
Of heroes brave and fate's design.

Whispers of lore on gentle breeze,
Echo through ancient, haunted trees.
From shadows cast, the stories rise,
Beneath the ever-watching skies.

In legends spun from golden thread,
The hearts of giants, the dreams of the dead.
With every stitch, the past we weave,
Imprinted in the nights we believe.

Through silken strands of midnight black,
The colors burst, there's no turning back.
A constellation of tales unfurled,
Where myths and reality blend their world.

So lie beneath this canopy bright,
And let the stars illuminate the night.
For every fabric, a story told,
In the hands of time, our dreams unfold.

www.ingramcontent.com/pod-product-compliance
Ingram Content Group UK Ltd.
Pitfield, Milton Keynes, MK11 3LW, UK
UKHW021454280125
4335UKWH00035B/547